22 Legal Mistakes You Don't Have to Make

A Guide for Start-ups, Small Businesses, & Tech Entrepreneurs

Sue Wang

Illustrations by Norwic Wred

Papervine Press

To the Success of Your Business

This is not a legal guide for dummies. This is a book for the brave, the hard-working, and the curious – for people who care passionately about the success of their business.

This is also a book for people who don't have all the time in the world, so we're going to zero in on practical tips and actionable advice. In particular, we'll focus on the issues that I get asked about again and again when I speak at entrepreneurial gatherings.

We'll also look at issues that nobody asks about, but everybody *should*. There's nothing worse than being blindsided by an expensive legal problem. Fortunately, law is a lot like medicine: good habits and early detection can save a mountain of bills and countless sleepless nights. In this little book, as a public health initiative for small businesses everywhere, we'll focus on:

- Simple ways to prevent future legal problems
- Common mistakes to watch out for
- Specific provisions that should be in your contracts
- What to do now, and what can wait

As an attorney, I've advised clients of all kinds, from tech start-ups to restaurants, from one-person consulting services to global energy companies, from three-buddies-with-an-idea to publicly traded corporations. You would be amazed at how much all of these businesses have in common. As your business grows, you'll pass through the same decisions and dangers that every CEO faces: you'll find money for your set-up costs, you'll put together a team of great people, you'll protect yourself from lawsuits, and you'll learn to negotiate like a champion.

At every step, you need to use the law to your advantage. All businesses operate within an invisible framework of law, and in these pages we'll go through many concrete examples of how legal questions play out in the real world. This book isn't intended to provide answers for every situation, but I hope you'll come away with a sense of how to ask the right questions.

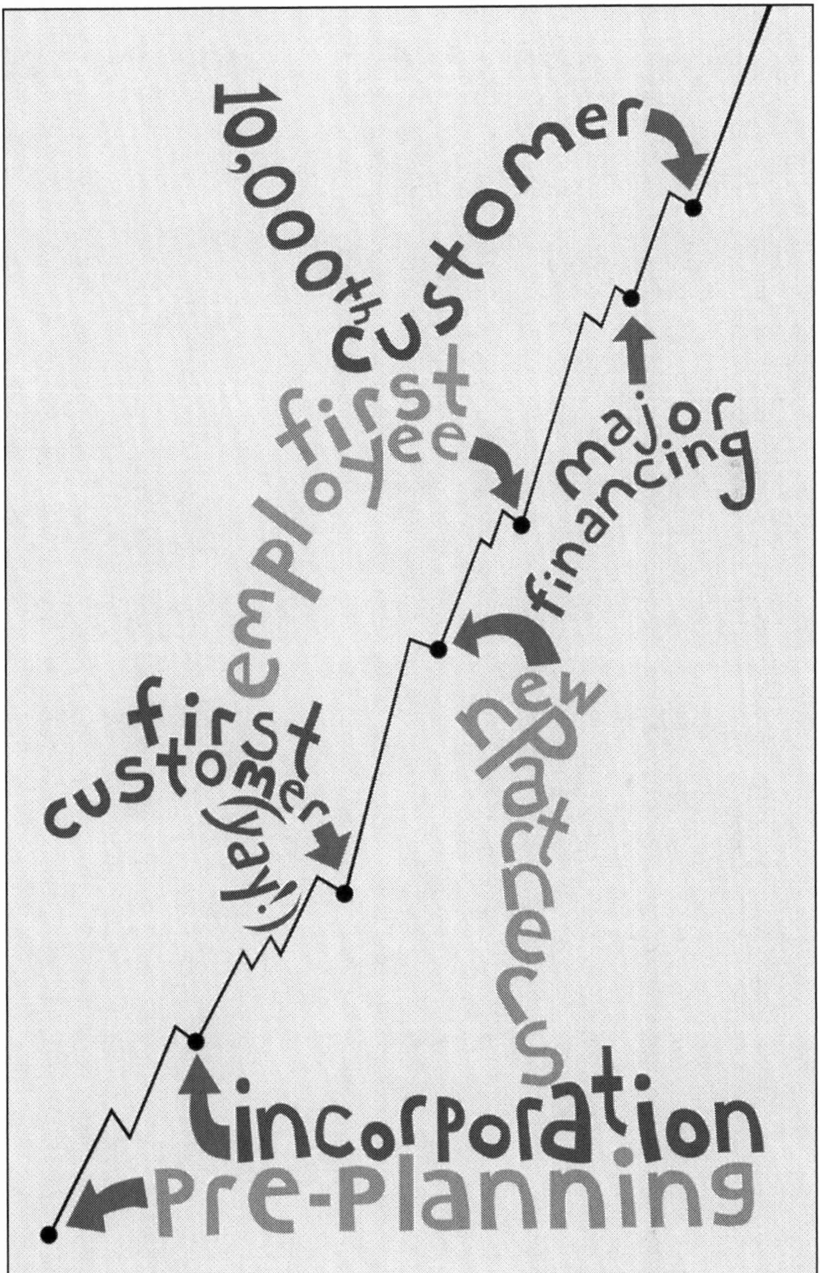

Pre-Planning
incorporation
first customer (yay!)
new Partners
employee first
financing
major financing
10,000th customer

Table of Contents

Money, or the Lack Thereof

Email Like a Pro

Get It in Writing

Lawsuit Repellant for Your Website

Confidentially Yours

Negotiate Like a Champion

How & When to Hire a Lawyer

Money, or the Lack Thereof

A careless beginning can have far-reaching consequences. I've known smart people who've personally guaranteed over $100,000 of corporate debt with one quick signature. I've also met entrepreneurs who weren't entirely sure who owned the company. This is dangerous: if a 3% share *might* have been granted several years ago as payment for services, there can be major problems down the line when that disputed 3% share could be the swing vote in a decision to sell the company or not.

Many of these problems happen because new entrepreneurs mistakenly go along with what they believe everyone else is doing. But in business, "everyone" is not doing the same thing. When it comes to start-up costs, the people with good lawyers do some very specific things.

{Mistake 1}

Giving away your company

So: you're just starting out and you need a website, a sales team, lawyers, and some people to manage the finances. Set-up costs can pile up long before your first paying customer arrives on the scene, so most companies start out "cash poor, equity rich." (Equity means stock, stock options, shares, and basically every other way a person can own an interest in a company.)

Whom should you pay with an ownership stake in the new company? Sometimes people start out thinking, "I'll pay equity to anyone who'll accept it! It shows that they're excited about my vision, and they'll have lots of incentive to help build the business."

Unfortunately, being too generous with equity is one of the worst mistakes an entrepreneur can make. For one thing, experienced professionals don't value equity if it's being offered too casually. If you offer shares to me the first time we meet, you're probably offering shares to everybody. That tells me that you aren't serious. It also opens up your company to unnecessary legal risks.

Danger alert: Too many shareholders

Any shareholder, even someone who owns just one share of stock, is anointed under the law with an ironclad set of rights. The law goes to quite a bit of trouble to make sure that minority shareholders don't get steamrolled by majority shareholders. In the eyes of the law, a person who bought one share yesterday has most of the same rights as a founding CEO who built the company while living on peanut butter and sleeping in a box.

In particular, all shareholders have a right to review your financial information at any reasonable time. Public companies do this by issuing annual reports that they file with the SEC. Smaller companies don't have to prepare special reports, but their shareholders generally have a legal right to show up at headquarters during business hours and literally look at the books. If you think about the possibility of shares being sold to a competitor, or the possibility that one of your shareholders could *become* a competitor in the near future, this should send shivers down your spine.

Moreover, shareholders have special rights to sue your directors and officers. If you paid Salesman Dan in equity three years ago and now he feels like you unfairly passed him over for promotion, Salesman Dan can cause a mountain of trouble. He might not win his lawsuit, but he can make you spend an enormous amount of time and money defending it. He'll also have unique access to dig through your records looking for evidence that can help him make more trouble.

Remember, people might not be interested in suing you now, but money attracts lawsuits. Let me say it again: Money attracts lawsuits. You don't want to slave away for years, hit the big time, and then get hit by big legal headaches.

Then there's the sheer paperwork. Someone has to keep up with the share registry, and all these shareholders might need to file profits and losses with their tax returns. If you filed for incorporation with an online service, it's likely that your corporate documents don't contain any restriction on share transfers. What if you have dozens of shareholders, who then transfer their shares to more

shareholders (one of whom is a competitor who now gets to look at your finances)? They wouldn't even have to let you know when they transferred the shares, unless your legal documents specifically require it.

Cookie-cutter legal documents are particularly dangerous because shares can be transferred by operation of law, such as in cases of death or divorce. About 30% of marriages end badly, and about 100% of people end eventually, so be aware of how these events can affect your business. For example, when Elon Musk, the CEO of Tesla Motors, filed for divorce in 2010, his company amended its SEC filings to explain how his shares were legally protected and why the divorce would not affect control of the company. Tesla Motors had accepted a loan from the Department of Energy, and the loan would go into default if the CEO's personal share ownership dropped below a certain threshold. In other words, Elon Musk's private divorce had become a public matter that could affect every shareholder who bought TSLA stock on the NASDAQ. Strong legal documents always close off the risks of automatic share transfer with carefully worded restrictions.

While you are small enough to be a closely held company, take advantage of the many benefits of being closely held. Restrict those share transfers and keep everything close. Over the next ten years, if your legal documents aren't far-sighted about restricting share transfers, you could end up with a host of unexpected problems: an ex-spouse with significant voting control, a hundred shareholders to keep track of, and uncertain ownership records.

Those are just the downside risks. Equity abuse also limits your upside. Obviously, as a matter of math, there's less equity for you. Less obviously, it can limit your ability to grow or sell your company many years down the line.

Don't limit your exit strategies

Imagine that Warren Buffett is interested in investing in your company. You've put in years of hard work, and you show Mr. Buffett around proudly. He looks at your financials, which are great. He talks to your customers, who are loyal. Then his lawyers look at your legal documentation, and they frown. They pull Mr. Buffett aside and whisper, "These people are amateurs, and there are any number of disgruntled ex-employees who could be minority shareholders. Buyer beware!"

Mr. Buffett lowers his offer price but decides to invest anyway. As you prepare to do the deal, you realize that your corporate documents require a 100% shareholder vote for mergers and major financings. That's unfortunate, because Salesman Dan is going to vote against the Buffett deal unless you buy back his shares for some serious cash. One holdout can have the power to torpedo your entire deal.

Even if you don't have a Salesman Dan to plague your nightmares, having a lot of scattered shareholders can cause severe delays. If you gave equity to the person who designed your first logo six years ago (and you aren't even using that logo anymore), are you sure you can find that person to get her signature? What if one of your shareholders passed away without a will, and now you have to spend time and money finding his heirs? In practical terms, enough delays can kill a deal.

Equity is a weapon, so grab it by the handle

Now that you understand the horrors of equity abuse, how should you use equity wisely? After all, equity is one of the most powerful weapons in your arsenal. There are many ways to deploy equity successfully:

Selectivity. First, think of equity as partner track. It should be a lot like tenure track at a university – you are essentially never going to fire someone who holds equity. Figure out how much time you need to work with a person before you can decide if they are permanent or not, and then negotiate a vesting schedule accordingly. For tech companies, the most common policy is a 4-year vesting period with a 12-month "cliff." This means that it takes 4 years to become fully vested, but if you leave the company before working there for a full year, you leave without any shares at all.

Vesting schedules. Unless it's a one-person company, nobody should get equity on Day 1, not even the co-founders. Since somebody needs to own the company, the practical way to create a vesting schedule for the co-founders is to have a buyback right: if one co-founder leaves early on (or is asked to leave), the company can buy back all of that person's shares for $1. On a technical note, make sure your attorney helps you file an 83(b) tax election within 30 days so that your unvested shares receive the most favorable tax treatment.

Transfer restrictions. To stay closely held, make sure that transfer restrictions are included in your incorporation documents. Any sale or transfer should be automatically void unless it goes through a right-of-first-refusal procedure. This means that existing shareholders are offered the opportunity to buy the shares and (just as importantly) always know in advance when transfers are planned. You may wish to go one step further and specify that all new shareholders have to be approved by a vote of the existing shareholders, or else the transfer is void.

Non-voting shares. If there is a clear difference between major shareholders and everyone else, consider issuing non-voting shares. Non-voting shareholders get the economic benefits of equity, but the company can rest easy knowing that it won't have to find (and convince) dozens of people to provide their votes and signatures. You'll still have to keep up with the non-voting shareholders so that you can send them tax information every year.

Stock options. Rather than issuing actual stock, it might be preferable to issue stock options. That way, people get the economic benefit of being on the ground floor, but they stay off your books until they exercise their rights. This delays the hassle of having so many owners, at least temporarily. Since other shareholders' interests will be diluted when a stock option is exercised, be aware that you have an obligation to tell future shareholders how many stock options are out in the world.

When you work with equity, you are making changes to the very core of your company. Small differences in language can have dramatic impacts on ownership and control of the company, so be thoughtful as you read your legal documents. Out of all the topics covered in this book, this is the one that most requires an experienced and careful attorney.

Pro Tip: Be alert even if you're only signing away 1% of your company

Many people believe that they'll maintain control as long as they keep 51% of the shares. This isn't true at all: there are plenty of scenarios where the merest sliver of stock controls the whole company.

Ford Motor Company, for example, remains

---

family-controlled even though the Ford family collectively owns less than 2% of the company. Ford's corporate documents are set up in a way that grants disproportionate power to that 2% of family shares. Likewise, investor-funded start-ups often have complex control mechanisms that favor the investors. Some common methods of modifying control include setting up multiple classes of shares, supermajority voting requirements, election of certain board members, and distribution preferences.

Once you give away control, it can be impossible to get it back, so be careful what you sign. For example, it's common to see a provision where, if the investors put in $250,000, the first $250,000 generated by the company goes directly to reimburse the investors. Since many tech start-ups expect to make their money by selling the company, I've seen poorly drafted documents that simply say, "when there is a distribution to the shareholders, the first $250,000 will go to the investors."

This sounds *almost* right, but what happens if the company becomes profitable and the founders change their mind about their exit strategy? The investors who control the board can vote to distribute profits every week, since the first $250,000 always goes to the investors. It sounds unfair, but people really do lose control of their companies by signing away their rights.

{Mistake 2}

Signing a personal guarantee

The most uplifting thing I've ever done as a lawyer is win a refugee case. It was my first and only refugee case, and the statistics were grim: nine out of ten claims were denied. My client had been in bureaucratic limbo for years and, even though he was a college-educated professional, he was legally unable to work. By the time we met, my client had been reduced to sleeping on park benches. Today, he's on track for Canadian citizenship and has a good job. He has his life back.

By contrast, one of the most difficult things I have to do is say to someone, "I'm afraid you may have to declare personal bankruptcy over this." In your business, it's fair to risk your investment of time and money, but you should never lose your house or your family savings. Your business venture should not be able to take your life away and leave you on a park bench.

When a personal guarantee is involved, however, personal bankruptcy can come into play. The alarming part is that, for many of the personal guarantees that I've reviewed for clients, my clients weren't fully aware of the obligations they had taken on.

What is a personal guarantee, and how does it work?

When you open your corporate bank account, banks will often offer to make a business loan to your new business. But the bank isn't crazy: your new business has no credit history, so the bank will only approve the loan if you sign a personal guarantee. This means that you will use your *personal* assets to back up your *corporate* debt. This works the same way as co-signing a mortgage for your brother – if he fails to pay, they can immediately go after you for the full amount.

Without a personal guarantee, corporate debt will generally be dissolved if the business declares bankruptcy. Once someone has a personal guarantee with your signature, however, your house is on the line.

In terms of risk, there is not much difference between (1) taking out a bank loan backed by a personal guarantee and (2) making a personal loan to your business from your own savings. For example, if you need $25,000 in start-up costs, and your brand-new business has no credit history, a bank will probably only offer to make that loan to your company if you already have more than $25,000 in personal savings or in home equity. Suppose your business runs into trouble and can't pay on time – then the bank will call on your personal guarantee. If you don't have the funds in ready cash, you might have to take out a second mortgage in order to access some of your home equity.

Since the risk exposure is so similar, it's smart to look at the interest rates being offered and consider whether it's a better deal to take out the second mortgage in the first place, loan those funds to your company, and have your company pay interest to you, not the bank.

The dangerous part

People don't always realize when they are being asked to

sign a personal guarantee. The language can be genuinely confusing. For example, many guarantees state, "I personally guarantee this loan *to the extent of my position as a shareholder in the company.*" This is still a personal guarantee! The limitation means that you are guaranteeing a *pro rata* share of the debt (for example, 50% of the debt if you own half the company). It still comes from your personal assets.

One good way to tell what you're really signing is to look carefully at the signature block. When a person signs a document on behalf of a company, the signature block looks like this:

Log Cabin Construction, Inc., an Illinois corporation

X_____
Name: Abraham Lincoln
Title: President

If Abraham Lincoln signs personally as an individual, his signature block is simpler:

X_____
Name: Abraham Lincoln

When you sign for a corporate loan, your signature block should always look like the first example. The *company* name should be the first line. *Please don't accidentally take out a loan in your own name!* You should always be signing on behalf of your company, in your position as its President, CEO, Treasurer, or Signer-in-Chief.

The loan officer who handles your documentation isn't a lawyer (or if she is a lawyer, she's not *your* lawyer), so always check carefully and ask questions if anything seems unclear. Bring this book with you if you need to. At the end of the day, it's your signature that will be on the document, and it's your responsibility to make sure you don't end up bound to something you never intended to agree to.

{Mistake 3}

Skipping the paperwork
on family loans

For many new businesses, loans from friends and family can be the quickest way to get started. For example, if your mother is willing to lend $15,000 to your new company at 5% interest, that would be a great deal for everyone – your company would get an attractive interest rate, and your mother would get a better return than from her savings account.

Obviously you won't just take a check and deposit it in your corporate bank account (or worse, your personal bank account – keep them separate!). The right way to set up the loan is with a short legal document called a promissory note. This can be just one or two pages long, as long as it covers the basics: the date the loan was disbursed, the total amount, the identity of the lender (for tax purposes, it may be important to distinguish between mom and dad), the identity of the debtor (your company, not you personally), the interest rate, and the term of the loan (6 months, one year, 2 years, etc.). Unlike a mortgage, where you take out a big loan and pay it back on a monthly basis, your promissory note should specify that you intend to pay the entire debt in one lump sum on or before the due date.

The promissory note memorializes the loan and establishes a tax record for both you and your parents. When your company repays the loan, remember that the interest income is reportable.

But don't stop there.

If you have business partners...

Suppose you have two co-founders. If your mother is going to loan $15,000 to your company, is it fair to ask each of your co-founders to sign a personal guarantee for $5,000? YES. Your mother is no fool, and neither are you, so make sure that your business partners share in the risk of repaying the loan if the company isn't as successful as hoped. Anything less would be just plain unfair. If your partners aren't willing to sign a personal guarantee, the interest rate on that loan should be a lot higher than 5%, because that loan just got a lot riskier.

How to balance personal guarantees amongst partners

Whenever you're considering a personal guarantee, whether in favor of a family member or a bank or other lender, be thoughtful about the considerations below.

Your worst-case scenario. Are you and your partners each on the hook for 100% of the amount or for a pro-rated portion according to your share ownership? Unless the contract says otherwise, the default rule is that the lender can get 100% from whoever is easiest to find and sue. If you are the most creditworthy partner, that means that you will be the most likely person to pay. It's better to limit your liability to your share of the company.

Changes in ownership. If the obligation is pro-rated according to share ownership, is it fixed at the share percentage you own on the date you sign the guarantee, or does it change if your percentage rises or falls over time? Try to avoid situations where

19

you sign on for 50% of the liability, and then you bring in a new partner who has no exposure at all.

Repayment from company profits. If you're ever forced to pay on the guarantee, do you have a right to seek repayment from your company? You should have a brief agreement with the company that says, in essence, "If I, as an individual, have to pay for the company's debts as a guarantor, the company will pay me monthly out of its profits until the full amount that I paid (plus __% interest) has been repaid. No dividends or distributions may be made to any other shareholder until I am fully repaid." Maybe your company isn't profitable enough now, but you need to secure first dibs on income as it rolls in sometime down the road.

Rebalancing amongst partners. If multiple partners have signed personal guarantees (whether in favor of a family member or a bank), you should also have a short agreement amongst yourselves that regardless of who pays the bank, you will repay each other out of your personal assets so that the guarantee is split fairly. That way, even if the company goes bankrupt, you have a second line of defense.

Quick Question: What if my friends want to invest as a co-owner, not as a lender?

If your friends or family want to buy an equity stake in your company (for example, a $25,000 investment in exchange for a 10% ownership interest), the transaction becomes much more complex.

As we discussed in the chapter on equity, any change in the ownership of your company should be

---

managed by an attorney. Even if your family shares are intended to be non-voting, you'll want an attorney to make sure that the shares aren't transferable (including automatically due to death or divorce) and stay closely tracked. You'll also want to decide if company profits should be used to repay your friends-and-family investors first.

For example, if the company makes $50,000 in the first year, does the company pay $25,000 to your parents first and then distribute the remainder of the profits according to share ownership? Or, since your parents own 10% of the company, do they receive only $5,000 in that first year? The wording of your corporate documents can make a big difference.

{Mistake 4}

Falling for a scam

Scammers are like rats and roaches: They adapt quickly to new environments and can sniff out fresh food from a mile away. The latest generation of scammers has learned to target the business community. Here are three scams that my clients have asked about.

The foreign investor scam

Someday, you may receive an email that reads something like this:

From: Dr Mahmoud Saleh-Jur (MSalehJur@outlook.com)
Re: I am interested in funding [YOUR COMPANY NAME]

I am an investor who is ready to invest $70M and above in your sector, and I am favorably impressed by your business model. I can provide liquid cash and executive support for expansion and growth based on equity shares.

I am a director in Riyad Bank based in Saudi Arabia although this is a private investment

> that is not attached to Riyad. You can get
> more information about me here:
> www.riyadbank.com/English/AboutUs/
> BoardOfDirectors.html.
>
> I await your executive summary for review
> with my advisor.
>
> Many thanks,
> Dr. Mahmoud Saleh-Jur

Your first thought will probably be, "What a scam!"

Then, out of curiosity, you might do an online search for "Mahmoud Saleh-Jur." To your surprise, you find a LinkedIn profile with very impressive credentials. You also find some press coverage on the BBC, and you *know* the BBC website is secure. Moreover, you go to Riyad Bank and see Dr. Saleh-Jur listed on their Board of Directors. You do more research on Riyad Bank, and it really is a major bank in Saudi Arabia.

What's going on? This is starting to look legitimate! But why would a prominent Arab businessman want to invest $70 million in your tiny company? You start to wonder if there's some kind of U.S. law that restricts investment, and maybe the only way this guy can get in is via a smaller company.

That's when you call your lawyer, and she says, "Oh yes, we see this from time to time."

Dr. Saleh-Jur really *is* a prominent businessman in Saudi

Arabia, but he didn't email you. Some scammer set up a free account at Gmail, Outlook, or Yahoo, and now he's impersonating Dr. Saleh-Jur.

This scam is tricky because no entrepreneur wants to risk offending a real investor. Maybe Donald Trump really does hear about cool new business ideas and just send a note to the founders. Steve Jobs used to answer emails from random Apple users, after all. It's a long shot, but it could happen. Here are some red flags that should give you pause, however:

Email mismatch. Your investor's email address doesn't match his claimed affiliation.

Invisible friends. He mentions lawyers and advisors, but you don't hear from them. Real investors have attorneys, and good attorneys are disciplined about sending work emails from work accounts.

Deadline pressure. At some point, he starts giving you deadlines. Scammers always crank up the time pressure, hoping to trick their victims into a hasty decision. Be alert for statements such as, "My advisors have recommended an alternative investment, but because I have given you my word, as a matter of honor I will leave the decision to you for 24 hours."

The Chinese trademark scam

I get asked about the Chinese trademark scam more often than any other scam. The scammers have probably set up an automatic system every time someone reserves a domain name or submits a trademark application. Basically, the email reads like this:

> Dear Sir or Madam,
>
> We are a Trademark firm in Beijing, China. On August 29, we received JIUFA COMPANY's application to register [YOUR COMPANY NAME] as a Trademark in China. After auditing, we have found that this Trademark has been used by your company. Trademark Law requires Trademarks to be registered in each country. Please let responsible person contact us immediately. If we do not hear from you within 7 working days, we will go foward with Jiufa Company's application.

What this scam says, in somewhat garbled language, is that a Chinese company is about to register your trademark in China. (Similarly, the scammers might notify you that a Chinese company is about to register your domain name in China.) If you reply, they'll offer to register your trademark for a few thousand dollars, and then they'll run off with your money.

It's true that trademarks, like country-specific domain names, must be registered by country. If you actually do business in China, you would hire a Chinese law firm to handle the Chinese registrations. You would also register the Chinese domain names in order to publish a Chinese-language version of your website.

However, these emails aren't from legitimate professionals. It's just a scam, plain and simple. Think about it: If a licensed Chinese lawyer had a client who wanted to register a Chinese trademark similar to an existing U.S. trademark, would they want to alert you? Absolutely not. They would file as quickly and quietly as possible in order to secure their client's rights.

The fake invoice scam

One of the most subtle scams involves a fake invoice. It will be mailed via the paper mail, and it will look exactly like an official invoice from a corporate bureaucracy. It will come in an envelope with a window, and it will include a bar code for easy scanning, an account number with your company's name and address, plus lots of legalistic fine print. There may be a tear-off portion by the "Amount Due" section, and you'll be able to pay by check, by credit card, and even by e-checks and bank wires. The scam artists really make it very easy to fall for this scam.

The fake invoice often claims to be from an international trademark registry, and it'll charge you a few thousand bucks for filing fees. Or the fake invoice might be from a domain registrar who isn't actually *your* domain registrar: it's just a scammer trying to charge you again for services that you've already paid for with your real service provider. Sometimes the fake invoice will be marked as a "renewal," which is a cheeky touch since you never commissioned these fake services in the first place.

Fake-invoice scam artists are fishing for that 1% of companies where someone will write a $2,000 check due to confusion. Perhaps your bookkeeper knows you just filed a trademark and believes you need to pay anything official-looking. A moment of inattention could really cost you, so recognize a scam when you see one, and make sure anyone with access to your corporate bank account is alert as well.

Email Like a Pro

Perhaps you expected a legal guide to be all about contract clauses rather than tips on using email. We'll get to the contract clauses in later chapters, but miscommunication is the root of too many legal problems to list.

To cut through the fog of miscommunication, there's nothing quite so handy as email. It's fast, it's easy, and it has legal consequences. Here's how to use it to your advantage.

{Mistake 5}

Letting promises slip away

Who knows what it's like to live inside of someone else's head? There can be a disconnect between what you say and what people hear, and there can be an alarming disconnect between what people promise and what people later remember promising.

The art of the recap

Whenever you agree on something over the phone or in person, send an email afterward to confirm exactly what was said. I call this the art of the recap, and it is possibly the single best habit that you can develop if you aren't doing it already.

A recap email accomplishes a lot of things:

- Identifies the points that are agreed (and therefore closed).
- Identifies the next steps for open issues.
- Makes sure that what you said matches what they heard, and vice versa.
- Preserves a written record in case someone forgets or "forgets."

For example, when I was representing some potential investors in a multi-million dollar energy deal, we had a full day of meetings. As the investors' attorney, I took copious notes of all of the facts that were presented, as well as the timelines, anticipated

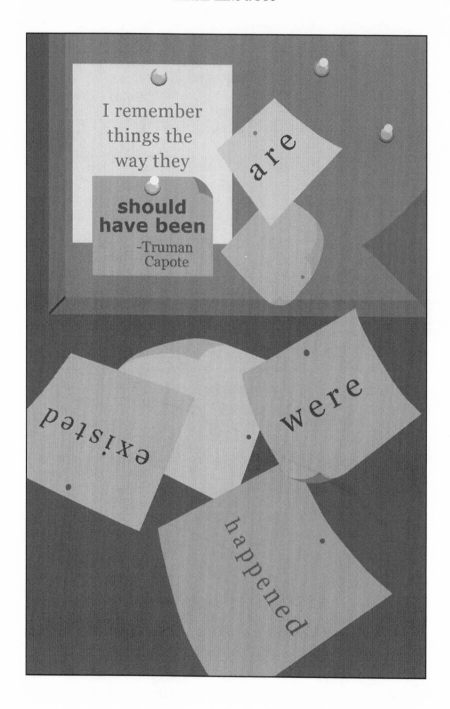

problems, and planned solutions. Once we got to the airport, my client turned to me and said, "Can you please prepare your notes for circulation to both sides?"

The next day, I sent my client some high-level notes. I covered the main points and some key details, especially where I privately thought the other company's promised delivery dates sounded a little optimistic. My client sent the notes to the company with a cover email that said, "This is our understanding of what was conveyed to us in yesterday's meeting. We covered a lot of ground yesterday, so please review these notes and let us know by the end of the week if we have misunderstood any portion of your presentation." This way, unless the company piped up with an objection, their promised delivery dates were on paper.

A sample recap email

It was great to chat today about the website relaunch. To sum up:

1. If we want to add API functionality, the August 25 deadline will be tight but do-able.

2. You'll re-size all the catalog thumbnails for us.

3. Re-sizing the thumbnails doesn't add any cost, but retouching the photos themselves will add 10K to the total cost if we want to pursue that option.

If this understanding is correct, I'll discuss with my team and get back to you. Please let me know sometime today or tomorrow if there is anything else you'd like to add.

Regards,
David

Notice that the example above explicitly states that it's a recap. It also gives a deadline for corrections (as opposed to asking for confirmation). Nobody can dismiss the email by saying, "Well, I never confirmed this summary, so it doesn't count." Finally, this recap takes the time to sum up the issues that are CLOSED (the first two items) as well as set out the next steps (the last item). This structure is important to make sure that closed issues stay closed.

Let's take another look

It was great to chat today about the website relaunch. **To sum up**:

> 1. If we want to add API functionality, the August 25 deadline will be tight but do-able.
>
> 2. You'll re-size all the catalog thumbnails for us.
>
> 3. Re-sizing the thumbnails doesn't add any cost, but retouching the photos themselves will add 10K to the total cost if we want to pursue that option. **(2 closed issues and one next step)**

If this understanding is correct, I'll discuss with my team and get back to you. Please let me know sometime **today or tomorrow** if there is anything else you'd like to add.

> Regards,
> David

If you aren't already in the habit of sending recap emails, give it a try after your next meeting. The basic formula is to summarize the main points, identify the next steps, and give a deadline for corrections.

{Mistake 6}

Mixing work and personal emails

Email can haunt you forever

Maybe I'll dress up as email next Halloween. Email can live forever, which is quite scary when you think about it. My emails live on my server, and also on the server of anyone to whom they were sent, cc'ed, or bcc'ed. If I hit "delete," it goes to the Trash folder, where it might live for another 30 days and get backed up 30 times. Other people might not delete it, and it could lurk unnoticed at the bottom of a long email chain.

It can also be forwarded to hundreds of people with the flick of a fingertip, and thousands more within minutes. Lawyers generally behave as if everything they say might be heard by the public, and in the internet age, that's not exactly paranoia.

As an attorney, I've sometimes reviewed people's entire inboxes. For example, a company will almost always start its internal investigations by scouring the emails on its own servers. When one company sues another, both sides are legally required to hand over all relevant emails during a process called discovery. If a business comes under investigation by any government agency, such as the SEC, FTC, DOJ, IRS, or any state-level equivalent, the company is expected to hand over copies of its hard drives with a whimper (meanwhile, the company will hire its own legal team to dig feverishly through the files in order to anticipate what the feds are going to find).

Sloppy habits can expose your personal communications

Like a lot of people, I have separate email accounts for work and personal matters. Unlike most people, my investigative experience has made me downright obsessive about keeping the two separate. Once you get in the habit, sorting work and personal email into separate bins is just as easy as putting the recycling or laundry into appropriate bins.

To be very clear: sending work emails through your personal email account does *not* protect them from searches — it just means that people will demand to review your personal email.

So what's the take-away lesson? Treat email with respect. Help everyone in your organization understand that *business emails are business matters*. An unwise joke or unfortunate phrasing can cause many sleepless nights (and high legal fees) under the right circumstances. On the other side of the coin, well-organized records can be the key to victory in a he said/she said situation years down the road. Email is a written record that lasts forever, and good habits will pay off.

Pro Tip: Don't go to prison because of email

Not only can email live forever, but you can even do hard time for intentionally deleting emails relevant to an ongoing or threatened dispute. The

---

moment you can foresee a legal dispute that is about to occur (even if the papers have not been formally filed in court yet!), all relevant emails magically transform into "legal evidence."

For example, if OSHA announces they're going to investigate your workplace safety, you can't go back and delete the email that says, "I'll bet you a pepperoni pizza that those brakes will seize up next month. I pity the poor suckers who are driving those crapmobiles." Destruction of evidence is a sub-category of "obstruction of justice," which is a serious crime. Obstruction of justice is what landed Martha Stewart in prison, so be warned.

{Mistake 7}

Changing your contract terms (or not) over email

For legal purposes, email counts as a writing. I know that "a writing" sounds like poor grammar, but this is how lawyers speak about evidence.

However, email is not generally considered to be a *signed* writing. There are electronic signatures now, but that's a different thing from regular old email. Generally, communications can be broken down into categories of (1) verbal communications, (2) unsigned writings like emails, and (3) signed writings like blue-ink originals, e-signatures, electronic PINs, and scanned or faxed signatures.

Technically, even verbal contracts are binding. "Binding" refers to whether an obligation would hold up in a court of law, as opposed to the many situations where people choose to follow through on their word as a matter of honor or good customer service. Verbal contracts have legal power because the laws of contract trace their roots over thousands of years. For most of human history, most people didn't read or write, but farmers and tradesmen still needed to do business. Thus if you offer your neighbor's kid $100 to help you paint the kitchen, and he agrees by hollering over the fence, you owe him $100 and he owes you a day of labor.

However, in a business context, you'd be crazy to rely on a verbal contract: it can quickly collapse into a he-said/she-said situation, and you'll be up to your eyeballs in legal fees before you see a dime in compensation. An email exchange is somewhat similar: maybe you created a binding contract, but maybe not. The rules of contract are complex (a thousand years is a *long* time to come up with legal theory), so you could rack up a lot of legal bills arguing whether an offer was made and accepted, as opposed to being met with a *counteroffer*.

In real life, we negotiate over email and close the deal with a contract

For businesses, a signed contract is the only sure way to show that both parties intend to change their legal obligations to each other. Once the signatures are on the dotted line, it's clear that an agreement has been entered into, although there can still be disputes over what that agreement consists of.

Let's take a closer look at how contracts and emails affect each other. Most contracts contain an "entire agreement" provision that essentially says, "This contract contains our entire agreement and replaces all previous oral and written communications." Even if the contract doesn't say these words explicitly, it will often be treated as if it did.

The order of events is usually:

Phase 1: Informal negotiations. The parties discuss over email, in person, or on the phone.

Phase 2: Legal markups. One side produces a draft contract, and the parties edit it in 0 - 100 rounds of back-and-forth exchanges.

37

Phase 3: Execution of legal documents. Both parties sign the contract. Once this happens, all previous negotiations vanish. (Poof!) In the eyes of the law, only the final contract exists. If something's not spelled out in black and white in the final signed document, it does not exist.

Phase 4: Living with the contract. After signing, the parties may choose to modify their agreement. This is where email might come into play.

Can you amend your contract via email?

Many contracts will need minor modifications over time (a change in a delivery date, an adjustment to the service fees, etc.). When you need to make a change, check your contract to see how amendments work. Does the contract say "amendments must be in writing" or "amendments must be in writing and signed by all parties"? In the first version, email counts as an amendment because the contract says nothing about signatures. In the second version, you need a scanned or faxed signature.

If you're going to be late in paying a vendor, for example, and their customer service person says "Don't worry about the late fee," that's not legally binding unless your contract allows for verbal amendments, which would be highly unusual. The company might stand behind what their customer service person says, but they have no legal *obligation* to do so.

To be legally binding, changes need to be made by someone who has the authority to change the contract (usually an officer), and the changes need to be in the appropriate form (oral, written, or signed) specified in the contract. If it's a $25 late fee, a customer service phone call is fine, but if it's a $5,000 late fee, be sure to get it in the right kind of writing signed by the right kind of representative.

Get It in Writing

As Joan Rivers once jested, the thing about washing the dishes is that you have to wash them again six months later.

Lax corporate housekeeping doesn't literally smell bad, so it's easy to let basic tasks build up until the dishes are teetering in hazardous piles. Let things slide for too long, and everything grows a fuzzy layer of mold: How many shares did we actually give to those employees three years ago? Which version of the joint venture agreement did we sign? Does that guy who left last year still have access to the corporate checking account?

Having a solid legal record is a highly cost-effective way to protect yourself from future headaches, and it's not hard once you get in the habit.

{Mistake 8}

Letting legal records get out of control

Things start out simple, but they don't stay simple. Today your company might be three buddies with a great idea. Over 10 years you might easily have over 50 friends, family, employees, and investors owning pieces of your company.

So do everyone a favor and keep decent records. Off the top of my head, here's a short list of some people who might get angry about haphazard records:

- Yourself
- Your lawyer and accountant (and yourself, after you see the extra fees charged by your lawyer and accountant to clean up the mess)
- The IRS
- The SEC
- Potential investors
- People who are your shareholders
- People who think they are your shareholders
- People who know they aren't your shareholders, but choose to claim to be shareholders just because they hate you, and they know you keep sloppy records

Keep a big binder of Lawsuit Repellant

How does one go about setting up a good record-keeping system? It's quite easy. As a bonus, it's also quite inexpensive in terms of both time and money. The time that you put into maintaining good records (as long as you don't go overboard) will often save ten times that amount of time later.

There's no need for special supplies, printed labels, fancy handwriting, or anything like that. All you have to do is follow these simple steps:

Step 1: Get a binder (cost: $1.99).

Step 2: Label it "LAWSUIT REPELLANT" (cost: $0).

Step 3: Inside, put signed originals of every document that changes your company's legal status or ownership details.

Step 4: To protect against theft or fire, scan every piece of paper in your binder and email it to yourself and your attorney (cost: $0 if you own a scanner, maybe $10 if you have to go to the copy shop).

Step 5: Put the binder in a safe place, maybe right next to where you keep your birth certificate and social security card. This binder, for all intents and purposes, contains the birth certificate and social security card of your company. Every time something happens legally (you sell some shares, grant some stock options, etc.), put a signed original in your binder (cost: $0). Remember to save a scanned version as well.

If you've gotten off to a bad start, either chase down the signed versions or get fresh signatures. Today. Do it today! Unsigned documents prove nothing.

What kinds of documents are we talking about?

Here are some examples of corporate documents that should be tracked. Each of these relates directly to the identity, legitimacy, and ownership of your company:

- Your certificate of incorporation in your home state (this is like your company's birth certificate)
- Your federal EIN (essentially your company's social security number, though there's no physical card)
- Foreign registrations in any other jurisdictions where you operate (as used here, "foreign" includes other U.S. states, not just other countries)
- Business licenses
- Your Articles of Incorporation (for corporations) or Articles of Organization (for LLCs)
- Your by-laws and/or shareholder agreements (for corporations) or your Operating Agreement (for LLCs)
- Your shareholder register (and keep this up to date every single time a share is issued or transferred)
- Share certificates and any accompanying stock powers (applicable only if your shares have a physical format)
- Signed resolutions from each year's annual shareholder or member meeting, and any annual Board of Directors meeting
- Any other board resolutions or corporate documents, such as minutes from Board meetings

You'll also want to keep tabs on your contracts with external parties. Once a contract is final and signed, take two seconds to park it in a designated spot so that you don't have to shuffle through draft versions when you need to check a provision. If it's a crucial contract, such as a $60,000 service agreement with a hospital, make sure you have both a hard copy and an electronic copy, and always remember that unsigned documents prove nothing.

Pro Tip: If something looks like Lawsuit Repellant, put it in the binder.

The list above sets out the top-priority items, but once you start thinking about Lawsuit Repellant, lots of other things will come to mind. If someone gives you permission to post their testimonial to your website, for example, print it out and keep a hard copy. You never know when you'll want to refer back to these little things, and it can save you the trouble of rooting though your files later on.

In particular, if anything important happens on an email server that you don't personally control, print it out while you're thinking about it.

{Mistake 9}

Misclassifying employees & contractors

For your corporate tax records, you will need to issue a W-2 form for each employee and a Form 1099 for each contractor who received more than $600 that year. But amongst your team, who gets which form?

Just because the job title says "consultant" doesn't mean anything. The IRS can and does look behind the label to the actual job function, so a misclassified person can lead to penalties and fines.

Same job, same pay, different tax status

The IRS has slightly fuzzy rules for determining whether a person is really an employee or not. Essentially, imagine a spectrum with a standard office worker on one end and a hired-gun freelancer on the other. Both can produce the same end product, but one will be an employee and the other will be a contractor. Let's say you need part-time marketing help, and you can hire either Emilio the Employee or Conan the Contractor. They're both going to do market research for you, at the identical hourly rate, but here's how they're different:

Supervision and independence. You ask Emilio the Employee to come in on Tuesdays and Wednesdays, and he's

48

expected to wear business-appropriate attire. Both Emilio and Conan are going to deliver a 20-page report on key market demographics for your product, but Emilio works under supervision while Conan works...in his pajamas? Maybe Conan emails you from his Italian villa. Maybe he lives on an island shaped like a skull and plots the destruction of the world when he isn't doing market research. You don't really care what Conan is up to, or where and when he does the work, as long as you get a 20-page marketing report and Conan picks up the phone when you call him.

Permanence. Emilio earns regular paychecks and expects to stick around for a while. When he's done with this report on market demographics, he'll start putting together new marketing strategies for you. Conan, on the other hand, is a fee-for-service kind of guy. If you're pleased with his work, you might ask him to produce a 50-page report on your competitors' marketing strategy, but then again you might not. If you do, you'll negotiate a new fee for the new service.

Exclusivity. Emilio's work is almost exclusively with you. If he's part-time, maybe he has two part-time jobs. With Conan, you are one among many in a portfolio of clients. Even if you are Conan's first and only client right now, Conan is working on further client development.

Profit and loss. Emilio earns a regular paycheck with a bit of bonus thrown in. Conan, on the other hand, is a business owner in his own right, and he stands to lose money if he under-quotes the project price or has to re-do the work.

Tools and materials. Emilio works in your office. When he prints his report, he prints it on paper that you bought, on a printer that you own. Conan, on the other hand, works on his own computer and has his own printer and paper.

Documentation for Conan the Contractor

Hopefully, this makes it relatively clear how your team members should be classified for tax purposes. If any position is ambiguous, consider: Can you comfortably increase the level of autonomy so that the position becomes a contractual position? The record-keeping burden is much lighter for independent contractors, which makes them a better fit for resource-lean start-ups. Basically, you'll need up to three documents:

W-9. For everyone, a one-page W-9 form, which certifies basic eligibility to work legally in the US.

Form 1099. For each contractor paid more than $600 in the current calendar year, you must file a Form 1099 with the IRS and send a copy to the independent contractor. This is to make sure that the contractor reports all of his income correctly.

A signed contract. For any contractor who does work of significance, you should sign a written Service Agreement. This can be just one or two pages but should be more detailed if they will handle confidential information. In addition to the compensation and service description, it should contain a "relationship of the parties" clause that explicitly says the team member is a contractor, not an employee.

Documentation for Emilio the Employee

If your company has any Emilios, you will need to have your paperwork checked over carefully by an accountant or human resources professional. In addition to Social Security and Medicare payroll taxes, you have to worry about workers' compensation taxes, unemployment insurance, and various other state-specific taxes and fees. Ignorance of the law is never an excuse, so seek out professional support on this one.

{Mistake 10}

Signing legal documents incorrectly

As we discussed in the section on personal guarantees, it's important to know when you are signing in your individual capacity versus signing for your company. It only takes a moment's inattention to create a legal error that has far-reaching consequences.

Always sign on behalf of the company

Suppose Abraham Lincoln wants to buy a truck for his construction company. He goes to the dealership and negotiates the sale and the terms of financing. After agreeing on a price and interest rate, the sales associate prepares a small stack of documents.

Lincoln reads carefully before he signs, and on the last page he notices this:

X_____
Name: Abraham Lincoln

Because Lincoln is a lawyer, he knows there's been a mistake. This new truck is meant for company purposes exclusively; for insurance and tax reasons, Lincoln wants the vehicle title to be registered in the corporate name. He also wants the financing to be a debt burden on the company, not himself, so Lincoln corrects the signature block to read:

Log Cabin Construction, Inc., an Illinois corporation

X_____
Name: Abraham Lincoln
Title: President

Easy!

Is one signature enough?

Now suppose Lincoln is in business with a foreign investor, Mahatma Gandhi of India. Although Gandhi only owns 5% of the company and has never stepped foot in Illinois, Gandhi is a lawyer as well,[*] and he knows how to protect his investment. Among other things, the Log Cabin shareholder agreement states that for any single contract or series of contracts totaling $10,000 or more, both Lincoln and Gandhi have to sign together.

The truck costs more than $10,000, so the correct signature block for the company should read:

Log Cabin Construction, Inc., an Illinois corporation

X_____
Name: Abraham Lincoln
Title: President

X_____
Name: Mahatma Gandhi
Title: Vice President

---

[*] Gandhi studied law in London and became a member of the bar in 1891.

Lincoln signs on the spot, and Gandhi faxes his signature in. Now the truck has been bought, and the financing terms have been agreed to by the company.

> ### Quick Question: But isn't Gandhi's legal name "Mohandas Gandhi"?
>
> Gandhi was born as Mohandas K. Gandhi, but today most people call him Mahatma Gandhi. Mahatma means "Great Soul" and is a term of respect. Does it matter which name Gandhi signs under? Not under U.S. law. People can sign under their birth names, married names, pen names, stage names, or nicknames. It's all legally binding, so you don't have to check up on people's birth certificates to know that their signature has legal effect.

Always be 100% certain about who has the power to sign

If you are the only shareholder of your company, it's pretty clear that you are in a one-signature situation. If you have partners, however, you should be clear about the questions below:

Checks. When writing checks from the corporate account, what dollar threshold should require two signatures? Decide this and be sure to communicate it to your bank, as well as include it in your shareholder documents.

Contracts. For contracts, can one partner sign on behalf of the entire company? Yes or no, make sure that your shareholder documents reflect your decision.

Special contracts. Are there certain kinds of contracts, such as taking on loans or high-dollar-value contracts, that require different rules?

Titles. What is the official title of each person signing? If people have multiple roles (for example, if you are both a director and the treasurer), which hat are you wearing when you sign?

Corporate resolutions. In cases where there are numerous shareholders, it's not uncommon to require a corporate resolution signed by a majority of the shareholders or the board of directors, authorizing the President or CEO to sign on behalf of the company. Should you require this extra layer?

You'll find your current rules (whether you're currently abiding by them or not) by reading your company's constitutional documents. Your constitutional documents are like the top of the box in a game of Monopoly. Usually, in the Operating Agreement (for LLCs) or the By-Laws and Shareholder Agreement (for corporations), there will be sections entitled "Members," "Managers," "Officers," and/or "Directors." These sections will say who has signature authority under which circumstances, and you should have your lawyer amend your documents to make sure they reflect the kind of signature authority that makes sense for your business.

For example, Washington Lumberyard, Inc. might have By-Laws that specify "any two directors may sign documents on behalf of the company." If that's all it says, then no meetings or board resolutions are necessary. The directors don't even have an obligation to tell anyone else in the company. As long as two directors' signatures are on a document, that document is valid. Their titles should each read "Director."

Roosevelt & Roosevelt Park Service, LLC might be more specific. Suppose its Operating Agreement says, "any officer of the company may sign contracts or documents for amounts up to and including $5,000. Contracts or documents for amounts over $5,000 must be authorized by a resolution of the board of directors and signed by two officers." If Eleanor Roosevelt, the company's vice president, wants to order $2,200 in new landscaping equipment, does she need to clear it with any other person? No. If she wanted to buy $5,001 of new equipment, she would need a board resolution and a second signature, but Eleanor can authorize $2,200 all by herself. She doesn't even have to tell any of her partners.

{Mistake 11}

Assuming the other party's signature is valid

Clever readers might be thinking, "What if I sign invalidly on purpose? Then I can follow through if I want, or I can repudiate the contract if I get a better deal elsewhere." While that works in theory, what will really happen is (a) people will think badly of you forever, and (b) if the contract is worth anything, people will sue you for misrepresentation. You might win, you might lose, and you will definitely pay your lawyers a large sum of money. For the most part, invalidly signed contracts just cause a big headache for everyone involved.

That said, it pays to be aware of the possibility that the person you're dealing with doesn't have authority to act on behalf of their company. For example, many otherwise well-run family businesses are plagued with one or two wild cards. Just because someone drives a company car and shares the family name doesn't mean that that person is authorized to bind the company. Likewise, if you are negotiating a major revenue contract with a hospital, it's important to know whether the person you're dealing with has cleared your deal with their internal approval process.

For most small business situations, people check for authorization by politely asking the other side if all approvals have been obtained. For example, you might write to your contact at the hospital, "Looking ahead, are there any internal approvals that you need to shepherd this through before we can both sign off on this agreement? We're happy to provide any support that would help speed along the process."

Company seals don't necessarily mean anything

Sometimes people think there's no need to check up on the other party's authorization if the other party's signature page has a fancy-looking seal or an inscription by a notary public.

Seals and notaries do not necessarily mean anything. You can buy a custom-made seal at any office supply store for about $50, and in all my years of practice, I have never known a single company whose documents said that the seal authorized documents by itself. Sometimes the requirement is "signature plus seal," in which case you still have to check that the signature came from an authorized person.

In other words, if a well-dressed woman from a prominent business family drives up in the company car and wants to order $100,000 in equipment, but you smell alcohol on her breath, it pays to check with the company's central office before you do anything that puts you out of pocket. The fact that she stamps her shaky, alcoholic signature with an engraved seal doesn't mean a thing.

Notarization establishes identity, not signature authority

What exactly is a notary public? Until I went to law school, I was a little confused about this too. A notary is a person who checks the government-issued ID card of a person before he or she signs. Then the notary watches that person sign the document. That's all.

The notary is registered with the state, so if it turns out that an imposter signed something, the notary can be tracked down and blamed. This means that having a notarized signature makes it all but impossible for somebody to later say, "I never signed that." Some notaries have engraved seals and some don't. Again, the seal comes from the office supply store.

Lawsuit Repellant for Your Website

For some brick-and-mortar businesses, the website is just one piece of a larger marketing strategy. For tech start-ups, the website can be 90% of the business.

When I look at a website as an attorney, however, what I see are opportunities: opportunities to sue.

Let's close off some of those opportunities, shall we?

{Mistake 12}

Copying someone else's privacy policy

Most people believe that privacy policies are there to protect the consumer. That's partially true, but attorneys look at privacy policies as a tool to protect businesses.

Why? Because a privacy policy provides certainty.

If you don't have a written privacy policy, you still have obligations – but it won't be clear what those obligations *are*. When a customer gives you information, what is their expectation? If you don't spell out your policy beforehand, customers have a legitimate right to sue you over what you *should* have done to protect their information, and you can argue for a long time about what was reasonable under the circumstances. More likely, you'll settle the suit just to make the complainers go away. Multiplied by many complainers, that can cost you serious money.

If you post a privacy policy, the doctrine of "informed consent" kicks in and protects you. By publicly posting information about how you collect and use information, whom you share it with, whether you sell it, how you protect it, and so forth, you essentially create an "Enter at your own risk" sign. Anyone who doesn't like your policy can leave. As long as you follow your own policy, customers can't claim that they got into something unexpected.

Practical tips for a smart privacy policy

Your privacy policy should be tailored to your specific business and how it actually collects and uses personal information. Here are a few tips:

Don't get carried away. Sometimes I see marketing copy that says things like, "Your privacy is our top priority" or "We use state-of-the-art technology to protect your information." These are not empty promises! Courts have held that a company can increase its own responsibility by throwing around language like "top priority." Is your top priority to safeguard your customers' sacred privacy, or to make money? How does your state-of-the-art security compare to a bank or a military contractor? If you don't have the best security money can buy, don't claim to have the state of the art. You can convey the same idea by saying, "We care about your privacy."

Reserve the right to change the policy without notice. Whatever you envision for your company right now, there might be changes that become vitally important in the future. Make it easy on yourself by explicitly stating that your policy may change without notice and that customers should revisit the policy from time to time. This might sound shady, but it's pretty standard amongst company policies. Chasing down your users is just too hard (and plus, 99.99% of your customers hate to get mail about your fine print).

There's no need to talk about the future. People like to say "We'll never sell your information" because it seems friendly and non-threatening. But...*never* ...is... a... long... time. Two years from now, you might get hit by a patent lawsuit and have to close your business altogether. If that happens, your user database could be

64

one of your most important assets, and you'll want to sell it to your next company so that you can start over. Or maybe things will go swimmingly, and you'll want to start a new company in a related industry and have access to that great mailing list that you worked so hard to build. If you need to, you can decide on a respectful way to use the data at that time, so don't preemptively cut off your legal rights.

Resist the temptation to cut and paste someone else's privacy policy. I can always tell when someone has done this because the resulting privacy policy makes no sense. It will usually leave out important bits, such as what happens to uploaded videos, or it will include irrelevant bits, such as provisions about information that you don't actually collect. It's worth spending a few hundred dollars to discuss your information use with an attorney and customize a legitimate privacy policy. The attorney might have some useful insights on how you're using the information, too.

Be extra careful about children under 13. First, children don't have the legal capacity to enter into contracts, so your fine print cannot bind a child who accesses your website. Second, there is a very strict set of legal requirements governing the privacy of children. A website is not allowed to collect so much as a child's *name* without parental consent. (If you look closely at Amazon, for example, you'll notice that some reviewers are identified only as "a kid." Amazon can afford lawyers, so they know that they can't collect and display a child's name.) There are ways to work within this framework, but unless your site is oriented toward kids, be wary of allowing any users under the age of 13 to give you any information at all.

Make it easy to unsubscribe. If you intend to send commercial emails of any kind, you have a legal obligation to have a functioning unsubscribe mechanism. This can be a web interface or an email address where people send requests, but it has to exist and it has to actually work.

Be aware of your legal obligations

For most legitimate businesses, the main effect of the CAN-SPAMM Act of 2003 is that unsubscribe mechanisms are mandatory and must be included in every single message. If you have any unusual plans for guerilla marketing where you might use a false sender name, include adult content, or harvest email addresses from the internet, you should consult an attorney about the rules of CAN-SPAMM.

Also, because of ongoing concerns about identity theft, there are new laws that are starting to be enacted at the state and federal levels, requiring businesses to protect certain types of personal information like social security numbers, regardless of what your privacy policy says. This is an evolving field of law, so if you handle any kind of sensitive data, you should consult an attorney who is conversant in the laws of information and technology.

Quick Question: Isn't "informed consent" a medical term?

Yes. The doctrine of informed consent grew out of medical cases. Until more comprehensive privacy legislation is enacted, the courts have decided that informed consent is also the best way to think about privacy.

Basically, if a doctor removes your gallbladder without asking you first, we would call that "assault." The idea of informed consent arose after some patients claimed that, although they had willingly gone under the knife, they would not have done so if someone had explained their options more fully. For example, maybe a breast cancer patient would have chosen to remove only the tumor rather than the entire breast if her doctor had explained that both options were available.

As a result, the legal rule is that consent only counts if it is "informed consent." A doctor has to inform you of your options before he operates, and you have to inform your users about how you're going to handle their information before you collect it.

Missing an opportunity to prevent nuisance lawsuits

Nuisance suits can be more than a nuisance, and if you're an online company with 23 million users, there's a real possibility that at least a few of those users will be crazy. The goal is to stay out of court completely, not to spend thousands of dollars winning a case, so let's look at defensive measures to shut down lawsuits before they even start.

As they say, the large print giveth and the fine print taketh away. Here are some major features that should be included in most business's general terms. Your terms and conditions can be on your website if your business is based on the internet, on the back of your receipts or invoices if you sell something, or embedded as part of your basic customer contract if you're a service company.

Liability limits

If you are old enough to remember the days when people dropped off film for developing, you might recall that the photo envelope always had a little disclaimer: "If there is any damage or dispute, you agree that One Hour Photo's liability is limited to the replacement cost of the film." Translation: if One Hour Photo wrecks your priceless wedding photos, they will pay you $5 so you can buy another roll of film. This is legally valid.

Similarly, an answering service might say, "Virtual Receptionists is not responsible for any contingent losses or special damages such as lost business." Translation: if the answering service drops calls and loses your million-dollar client, they will refund you their monthly service fee of $200.

As a consumer, these terms might seem unfair at first. As a business owner, however, you can appreciate the necessity of these protections. One Hour Photo can't spend its time arguing over how valuable each photo is – it is so much easier to just declare that photos are merely worth the film they are captured on. Likewise, if you owned Virtual Receptionists, what would you do if you had delusional clients who believed that they were losing business due to your receptionists rather than their own shoddy product? It's best to limit your liability so that no one can even *claim* that you caused them to lose business. If they're unhappy with the service, those customers can take their business elsewhere.

Time limits

If you sell any kind of physical good, you probably already have a refund policy. But service companies should also specify a refund period: If your software development company doesn't spell out the time in which a client can bring up problems, you might get a call 10 months later about a new bug the client just found. Draw a bright line of 10 days or 30 days for them to test the product – for anything more, they need to buy the extended support package.

In addition to the refund period on your actual deliverable, you need to draw a line around all other claims. For example, what if one of your online customers wants to bring a privacy claim because her junk mail increased dramatically after she signed up for your newsletter two years ago? No way, right? Unfortunately, unless you specify otherwise, she probably can bring that claim. Each state has different rules about how long you can wait to bring a claim (the "statute of limitations"). The limits tend to be from two to five years for most civil claims. Major crimes can have limits of over a decade.

In your terms and conditions, be sure to limit all claims to a shorter period. In many cases, you can cut it down to 12 months and still be valid. (If your limitation is too aggressive, a court might invalidate it due to reasons of public policy.) This limitation runs both ways, so if you find out that a customer has been ripping you off for the past three years, you would only be able to recover for the last 12 months.

Jurisdiction

Being sued is not the worst thing that can happen; being sued by customers in all 50 states, filing separate lawsuits at their local courthouses, is the worst thing that can happen. Grab the bull by the horns and make your tormenters come to you. Choose one state and declare that the courts of that state have *exclusive* jurisdiction.

There are certain circumstances where a court may apply the law of another state (for example, if a divorce is filed in Indiana but 20 years of marriage took place in California). Prevent that headache by also declaring that the laws of your state will govern all disputes.

Who pays for legal fees?

Europeans are always amazed at the number of lawsuits that American businesses face. One big reason is the way American legal

fees work. In most other countries, the losing side has to pay for the winner's legal costs. That means that a weak claim can really backfire, so people are more cautious about bringing lawsuits.

In America, each side bears its own costs, with a twist: plaintiffs' attorneys typically represent clients on what's called "contingency." Contingency means that the client pays nothing up front, and the attorney will take around 30% of the settlement award. I say "settlement award" because most cases don't go to trial: defense attorneys have to be paid hourly rates of around $250-$600 an hour, so defending a case can be more expensive than losing a case. Many business owners feel compelled to settle even when they know they're in the right.

In your terms and conditions, you have the power to change the rules regarding legal costs. If you sell a $2 iPhone app, for example, you know you're probably not going to sue your customers. To discourage them from bringing claims against you, your terms and conditions should include a "loser pays" clause. Then whoever loses will pay the legal fees for both sides.

Reserve the right to change your terms

Just as with your privacy policy, it's important to maintain flexibility as your business changes. State that your online terms and conditions are subject to change at any time; your needs will change over time, and so will the law. When these things happen, you aren't going to chase down all 23 million people who have ever visited your website.

The limitations of the fine print

The tools we've discussed here only apply if there's a

contractual relationship between you and your tormenter. Many lawsuits are based on contract, but many others are not, so the best-drafted contracts in the world will not prevent people from suing you. For example, if a competitor sues you for copyright infringement, there's no contract between the two of you. If an employee sues you, a portion of the claim might be based on your employment contract, but other portions of the claims might be based on state minimum wage laws or federal safety requirements. In that case, your terms and conditions would only apply to the contractual portion of the dispute. These protective contractual provisions are like a shield for your torso, not a full suit of armor.

{Mistake 14}

Wasting time and money in a jury trial

Once you start really looking, arbitration clauses crop up the same way that Paul Rudd seems to be in every movie made in the last 15 years. "Arbitration" is the legal term for opting out of the public court system in favor of private dispute resolution (also called alternative dispute resolution or ADR). Basically, it's a way of running your own mini-trial. Why is it so popular?

Three reasons: time, money, and confidentiality.

As the years add up, so do the legal fees

Public courts often have backlogs of cases that run for over a year, and with the current slowdown in judicial confirmations, experts expect the backlogs to get much worse in the next decade or so. Once a case is filed, there's no hard limit on how long it can take. If one side has a big war chest, the lawyers can trot out one expert witness after another, make lots of motions, and generally drag out the process.

Then, once a verdict is reached, there is always the possibility of appeal. A good lawyer can find a lot of claims to hang an appeal on: that the trial judge misconstrued the law, that a piece of evidence was incorrectly included or excluded (see: O.J. Simpson trial), that the jury gave an unconscionably large award... the list

75

goes on. Requests for appeal can be accepted or denied, retrials can be ordered, and until all appeals are exhausted, the case is not entirely closed.

Not only can all this stretch out for years, but it almost goes without saying that the longer it lasts, the more money has to be spent by both sides.

Arbitration is not necessarily cheaper, but it often is. The parties can agree on a streamlined process. For example, each party might be permitted one written brief of up to 20 pages, five witnesses who may each be questioned for up to six hours, and a 30-minute closing argument. Both sides will still retain attorneys, but the process is shorter and therefore less expensive. Because of this, the total cost can be lower even though the parties have to pay for the services of a private arbitrator.

It's key to note that a good arbitration clause specifies that arbitration is binding and non-appealable. Whatever the arbitrator(s) decide, both parties must accept the decision as final. When you're done, you're *done* and everyone can move on. The winning side can go to any court having jurisdiction and present the arbitration judgment for enforcement. The *only* reason a court can decline to enforce an arbitral award is if the underlying arbitration clause is invalid. For this reason, arbitration clauses typically have an all-caps portion that reads, "EACH PARTY ACKNOWLEDGES THE ARBITRATION CLAUSE AND WAIVES ITS RIGHT TO A JURY TRIAL."

Court trials are usually public

Finally, there's the confidentiality issue. Many court documents are confidential, but important parts of trial are public. The list of cases on the docket, for example, is public. That means

that any journalist, employee, or competitor can see that your company is involved in a lawsuit. Most court trials are open to the public, meaning that anyone can stroll into the courthouse and have a seat. (In Washington, DC, you can even watch the Supreme Court.)

The judge's written opinion is public and becomes part of the scholarly fabric. It will stay publicly searchable forever, which can be remarkably embarrassing even if you win. For example, almost every law student in this country still learns about employment discrimination by reading the unflattering case of *Price Waterhouse v. Hopkins*. Although Ann Hopkins had landed a $25 million client account and was clearly one of the top performers in her class, the company chose not to offer her a promotion to partnership. One partner noted that although Hopkins was an outstanding performer, she needed to "walk more femininely, talk more femininely, dress more femininely, wear make-up, have her hair styled, and wear jewelry." All of this is in the public record because, in addition to laying out Pricewaterhouse Cooper's top-secret partnership selection process in great detail, the court opinion quotes directly from Hopkins's personnel file. Even by 1982 standards, it was embarrassingly sexist.

In contrast, a good arbitration clause usually specifies that arbitration will be completely confidential, regardless of who wins or loses. Even the fact that a dispute is being arbitrated at all may be kept out of common knowledge.

One potential drawback

Many attorneys believe the finality and confidentiality of arbitration are clearly superior to a trial at court. However, some attorneys complain that arbitrators often attempt to please both parties by issuing compromise decisions too often. There may be some truth to this complaint, although it's also true that, in many disputes, both parties actually *are* equally at fault.

Note that if you choose arbitration, you still need to pay attention to the issues of legal fees, jurisdiction, and choice of law that were covered in the previous chapter. In an arbitration clause, these are taken care of by stating where the arbitration will take place, which state's laws will apply, and that the losing side will pay legal fees unless the arbitrators rule otherwise. It's also useful to have a jurisdiction clause so that you'll know which court to go to, in case you need to enforce the judgment if the losing side refuses to pay up.

Who are the arbitrators?

In a court case, judges are public servants, and in theory you get whichever judge happens to take your case. In practice, attorneys sometimes engage in strategic maneuvers to try to get a certain judge, and jury selection is an art and science unto itself. In arbitration, on the other hand, the parties run the show, and they choose and pay for the arbitrator. For small cases, the parties usually jointly appoint one neutral arbitrator. For larger disputes, the parties often appoint a panel of three arbitrators. In those cases, usually each party nominates one arbitrator and then they mutually agree on a third Chief Arbitrator.

Arbitrators are often retired judges, who can make significantly more money as private-sector arbitrators than as public servants. They might also be senior attorneys or seasoned professionals in the relevant industry. Alternative dispute resolution is a well-established industry with clear rules of procedure, and ADR centers maintain rosters of approved arbitrators for you to choose from.

Quick Question: Are mediation and arbitration the same thing?

No. Both mediation and arbitration are increasingly popular due to cost concerns, but they are very different. Where arbitration is like a private court trial, mediation is like couples counseling. A private mediator will help both parties communicate and discuss potential compromises, but the mediator is never supposed to take sides or issue a decision. Instead, he or she helps reboot the discussion and brings a more professional and non-emotional tone to the dispute. If mediation fails, the parties will proceed to either arbitration or a court trial.

{Mistake 15}

Getting nabbed for copyright infringement

The first rule of blogging is that every post should have a picture, right? Magazine editors used to squint through paper catalogs of stock photography, but these days anyone can punch a few words into an image search and find the perfect graphic in seconds.

With a few clicks, you can upload the new picture to your website. Easy! Unfortunately, in those same clicks, you just exposed yourself to up to $30,000 of potential liability.

This sounds severe – it sounds downright outrageous – but the law really does establish a breathtakingly high ceiling on the penalties for copyright infringement, even for non-commercial use. Remember the Napster lawsuits where record labels sued ordinary people for astronomic sums? The music industry's public relations strategy has changed since then, but the law itself hasn't changed.

This is not a theoretical risk. Image searching has become much more sophisticated in recent years, so photographers can easily search for their own images to check for infringement. Some of the shadier stock photography companies might even be making it easier to rip off their wares – they can make more money by suing people than by actually selling images, video, or music. (At this point, some readers are revolted...and others are thinking, "Hey, that's a great business model!")

If you do a bit of research you'll find that people settle for thousands of dollars, not hundreds of dollars.

The unfortunate truth is that the law always lags behind technology. Historically, the law has sometimes led society and sometimes followed far behind. When *Brown v. Board of Education* declared school segregation illegal, the law led society. When it comes to internet and technology, however, the law follows... sometimes very far behind indeed.

"Fair use" doesn't mean what you think it means

We are living in a time of great transition, and an ethical consensus has developed on the internet. Most people, including many professional publicists, believe that it's okay to use an image, video footage, or music clip as long as (1) you aren't making any money from it, (2) you've credited the creators and linked to their websites, and (3) if a creator were to contact you, you'd take down the offending material immediately – no harm done.

This share-and-share-alike attitude *feels* very fair. It really does. You're not making money from it, so you shouldn't have to pay for it, right? Unfortunately, that's not the law. (If share-and-share-alike *were* the background rule, people would not have needed to establish Creative Commons licensing in the first place. More on that later.)

As far as the law is concerned, it doesn't matter if you make money from the infringement: infringement is infringement is infringement. And penalties are high. If you use someone else's photo, there are four main ways the story can end:

- You'll get lucky, because the photo belongs to someone who doesn't particularly care about who uses it (and maybe is even flattered). This is what will happen 99% of the time.

- You'll get lucky, because the photo belongs to a professional photographer who requests you to take it down, politely explaining that this is how he earns his livelihood.

- You'll get unlucky, because the photo belongs to an angry professional photographer who is tired of spending hours of his time policing Google Image Search, and he's contacted a lawyer who is willing to prosecute the lawsuits for a 30% share of all settlements, no payment up front.

- You'll get extra unlucky, because the photo was put on the internet as bait for unwitting victims, and you receive a letter from a stock photography company demanding $15,000 in immediate settlement if you want to avoid a lawsuit for $150,000.

You might feel like this kid right now...But don't worry!
I paid less than $10 for the right to use this professional photo.

"Tetons and the Snake River" by Ansel Adams (1942) is worth a lot more than $10, but it's completely free to use. You can use it, reproduce it, change it, and even sell it.

Most of Ansel Adams's work is covered by copyright, but this famous photo is part of the public domain because Adams was employed by the National Park Service in 1942.

A little-known fact about takedown notices

Most internet users believe that you can only be sued if you fail to respond to a takedown notice. "If someone asks me to take it down," you think to yourself, "I'll take it down immediately and apologize all over myself."

Unfortunately, although many rights holders issue a warning shot as a courtesy, there is no legal requirement to do so. The law is deadly serious about copyright infringement – it's presumed to be stealing the most precious thing a creator makes. If I stole your grandmother's wedding ring, and I gave it back immediately after you found me wearing it, you could still have me arrested.

The confusion arises because there *is* a safe harbor for companies like YouTube, which hosts user-generated content. YouTube can't be expected to know what its users are posting every minute of every day, so the Digital Millennium Copyright Act (the DMCA) created a safe harbor for any company handling user-generated content. If you run a website or message board where users post content, establishing a prompt takedown process can protect you from secondary liability for your users' actions. If you post content to your own corporate blog, however, there's no legal obligation for anyone to send you a courtesy note before they sue you.

Practical tips for using images safely

When you're putting together your website, your company blog, and other marketing materials, it pays to be meticulous about copyright.

- If you've purchased stock photography, keep a copy of each photography company's standard license agreement in a safe place and track your receipts. It's Lawsuit Repellant, just like your well-organized corporate records. Read the agreement so you know whether you need to pay more money each time you use the image.

- In America, works published prior to 1923 are in the public domain. Thankfully, the internet has plenty of archived works, including paintings and sketches by artists such as Rembrandt, Velasquez, Klimt, and Van Gogh. Why use cruddy cameraphone shots when you can class up your website with a Vermeer?

- Photos taken by government employees while on the job are in the public domain, regardless of when the photo was taken. The Library of Congress has a remarkably high-quality image collection and is one of my very favorite sources. (Not everything there is public domain, so always check.)

- One of the best ways to be sure of the copyright status is to use your own photos, or those of friends or family who have given you blanket permission. You probably know at least a few people who have massive collections of photos online.

- For musical recordings, be aware that each recording involves at least two copyrights: the composition and the specific performance. This means that you can't use the New York Philharmonic's performance of Beethoven, even though Beethoven's works are in the public domain. You also can't use your own rendition of "Hey Jude." (Famously, this is why restaurants no longer sing "Happy Birthday to You.")

- Likewise, for translations or other derivative works (such as a

87

photo of a Rodin sculpture), each aspect of the work has to be considered separately. Homer's Odyssey, for example, is three thousand years old, but the English translations are more recent. To comply with copyright law, Project Gutenberg offers the full text of Alexander Pope's 1725 translation and Samuel Butler's 1898 translation, but not Robert Fitzgerald's excellent 1963 translation.

- If you think you might fall within a "fair use" exception, check the rules carefully. Fair use is almost never as broad as people believe. Unless you're a book reviewer or a teacher (in the sense of being an actual schoolteacher, not in the broader sense that all non-fiction is educational), or you are creating a parody of the original work, it's unlikely that your planned use falls within the legal definition of fair use.

- Likewise, be alert when using works with a Creative Commons license: CC licenses come in several flavors, some of which are quite restrictive. If a CC license requires attribution, for example, be sure to give credit where credit is due. If a certain work is labeled for non-commercial use only, remember that your business is probably commercial.

Quick Question: Why don't bloggers get sued more often?

Because most bloggers don't have money! In the legal industry, we refer to people without assets (either individuals or companies) as "judgment-proof." If copyright owners go to the trouble and expense to sue a mom blog, they might win a judgment for $50,000 – but how are they going to get that money? We don't have debtors' prison or labor camps in this country.

Now that you understand the basics of copyright, you may start noticing that many blogs with significant advertising revenue either take their own photos or use image subscriptions from stock photography companies, just like traditional newspapers and magazines.

Confidentially Yours

     Every business creates information worth protecting. Technology companies are made of information, but so is every other company. Think about your favorite coffee shop: does it have a secret recipe or two? Does it want competitors or the public to know how much it's paying for coffee beans? Does it have a mailing list of loyal customers?

     Your information is valuable, and it's *yours*. Whether it's a secret recipe, a list of prospective sales leads, or a business plan that will change the world, let's protect it.

Using a confidentiality agreement that doesn't fit

If you believe the movies, there's a lot of corporate espionage going on. The spies are remarkably attractive, too!

In the real world, businesspeople are more and more aware that our economy is based on information. Every business walks the line between paranoia and collaboration, and smart businesses get it in writing. Confidentiality provisions can be written down as fairly brief freestanding agreements, or they can take up roughly one page in a larger contract. These would typically be between your company and other companies, but also internally between your company and your employees or contractors.

Every confidentiality agreement
has four moving parts

To take control of your decisions, understand the moving parts of every confidentiality or non-disclosure agreement (NDA). A well-drafted confidentiality obligation should provide clear answers to the following four questions:

Scope. What kind of information is covered? Does it cover all information not previously known or publicly available, or only information that is specifically marked as "CONFIDENTIAL" somewhere on the document? If the contract itself is confidential, that too should be specifically noted.

People. Whom can the information can be shared with? If you are disclosing highly sensitive information, you might choose to restrict access to people in a certain department (as opposed to the entire company), plus legal counsel. Because of attorney-client confidentiality, adding lawyers to the exception is both common and safe.

Purpose. What purposes can the information be used for? If you are providing design specs to a manufacturer, for example, it makes sense to state that the information may only be used to perform contractual services for you. They should not be permitted to use your design specs for any other horrible purpose.

Time. How long does the confidentiality restriction apply? Sometimes the confidentiality only runs for as long as the underlying contract, but in many cases the confidentiality obligation will run for an extended period of one to five years after the main contract has expired. In extreme cases, the obligation will run essentially forever, or the maximum period permitted by law. If the confidentiality obligations are inside of a larger contract, make sure your attorney specifies that these obligations will survive termination of the main contract.

Too much secrecy?

Confidentiality restrictions are usually symmetric, so don't automatically reach for the strongest version! For example, if the contract itself is confidential, you won't be able to show that contract to potential investors without first getting consent from the contractual party. Be thoughtful about what you really need in terms of protection – armor is heavy, and too much of it can slow you down.

Also, specifically within the tech industry, investors almost never agree to sign NDAs while they review a company. In Silicon Valley, the community is close-knit enough that people rely on reputations, and bargaining power is often severely lopsided, such that in certain situations even asking for an NDA can mark you as an outsider.

Quick Question: What's the difference between an NDA and a confidentiality agreement?

Some people will tell you that one is more about controlling the purposes that information can be used for, whereas the other is more about controlling disclosure to outside parties.

Here's a secret you should know: The title of the document doesn't mean much. It's just like a job title. We all know plenty of people whose jobs don't match their official titles at all. In practical terms, the main difference between the two is that "NDA" is shorter to type, especially on a mobile device.

{Mistake 17}

Letting the interns run wild

Information is a curious commodity: sometimes its value increases dramatically when shared, yet its value can disappear completely when shared with the whole world. Most people are alert to the need for confidentiality agreements with outside parties, but few start-ups have active policies internally.

Protect your trade secrets

Personal judgment varies widely, so your army of interns might not be aware that certain things shouldn't be talked about outside the company. It's great to have a written policy to go over with each new hire.

As a legal matter, having a written policy elevates your sensitive information to the status of being a *trade secret*. Entrepreneurs generally focus on patents, trademarks, and copyrights, but trade secrets have protected legal status as well. Trade secrets are legally protected from intentional theft by your staff and others, and their protected status never expires as long as you treat your information with care. Basically, the law will consider your information to be valuable if you demonstrate through your actions that *you* consider it to be valuable.

The law differs from state to state, but the general rule is that acquiring a trade secret through improper means or improperly disclosing a trade secret carries hefty civil (and even criminal) penalties. If you bribe a senior Coca-Cola executive for the secret formula for Coke Zero, for example, I guarantee that Coca-Cola Corporation will hunt you down, and the law will be on their side.

Practical tips for creating useful information policies

Your internal policy doesn't have to be written in legalese. It just has to answer the four questions covered by a confidentiality provision, in plain English. Your policy might say, for example: "None of the following categories of information (scope!) should be shared with anyone other than current officers, employees, or contractors of the company (people!) for any purpose (purpose!) at any time (time!), without the express written permission of at least one officer of the company." Then make a bullet-point list of the general types of your sensitive information, such as client lists, business plans, prototype designs, financial projections, and so forth.

If you are feeling energetic, there are plenty of other things your Confidentiality and Communication Policy can cover: best practices for encryption and security, sending work matters over personal email, non-disparagement in personal blogs and social media, how to respond to press inquiries, and whatever else you feel is worthwhile in your specific circumstances.

Once you have a policy, use it! Information control should be a continuing, active dialogue within your company. Be active about explaining the policy to every person involved in your company, and give them examples. Ask them if they can think of any additional information that needs to be protected. Cultivating a flexible, responsive culture of information-consciousness is your primary defense against unintended disclosures. With luck and preparation, you might never need to pull your legal weapons out of the armory.

Negotiate Like a Champion

The Spanish word for business is *el negocios*, and negotiating certainly is a major part of any businessperson's day. In this section, we'll look at the best ways to frame the business terms of your deal, plus how to protect yourself if things don't go according to plan.

Agreeing to terms that
are too vague

Speak the language of deliverables

When you negotiate a deal with someone, whether it's to hire a consultant, provide services for a client, or sell your entire business, you should frame the discussion in terms of deliverables. A good contract should have some measurable description of the goods or services.

For example, don't just hire a part-time marketing consultant to vaguely help you with social media. Get it in writing that Consultant Mark will spend at least 10 hours per week launching your social media campaign, and that his efforts should generate at least a 30% increase in your web traffic within three months. Laying out your requirements in terms of deliverables and benchmarks helps make sure that you and Consultant Mark have the same expectations, and it will keep him on the hook to deliver as promised.

Milestone payments and delivery

Whether you are the payer or the payee, you should be clear on how payments will work. It goes without saying that all payment discussions should be in writing. As an attorney, I'm also very careful to specify *when* payments are due. Once money leaves your hands, you have to go to court to get it back even if you clearly have a right to it.

Try to set up the timing of payments in a way that makes sense for everyone. For example, if you hire a company to build a mobile app for your business, you might pay a deposit upon signing the contract and release three milestone payments as they deliver a mock-up of how the app will look, a first revision based on your comments, and a second revision. You wouldn't pay the full sum until they deliver and install a fully functional product that you're pleased with.

Any business veteran can tell you that payments don't always happen on time (or ever, in some cases). Because of this, your contract should always say something about late fees and interest on overdue amounts. Not only does this compensate you if you have to wait 6 months for payment, but it also gives you the flexibility to say, "I'm just checking in because we haven't received your payment yet. If you could please check with your bookkeeper, we'll waive the late fee if we receive payment by _____."

Advocate for your own best interest

The instinct to be fair and evenhanded is very strong and generally admirable. In business, however, it sometimes isn't very smart. Certain terms can affect you more than the other party, and those terms need to be written with your particular interests in mind. It's a balancing act. You want a reputation as a fair and reasonable business partner, but there are limits. Don't negotiate against yourself.

Terms that seem to apply to both parties sometimes really

don't. For example, payment terms might seem evenhanded because, in theory, the seller would be subject to the same terms if they had to issue a refund. However, if you're buying a series of products, then a rule that "each party has seven days to pay any amounts due" is really mostly about you. Give yourself 30 days to pay so that you will have time to test the product. That way you can deal with the invoice paperwork only once a month and will have a bit of buffer in case cashflow gets tight.

Identify key pieces of the deal that fall on you, and set them up to your advantage. Consultant Mark's deliverable of a 30% increase in web traffic is a black-and-white number, but sometimes the deliverables can't be fully captured in numbers. If there's a judgment call to be made about whether a product is acceptable or a particular benchmark was met, begin by giving that decision to yourself.

Try to think ahead to the future and protect your own options. For example, if you're contracting to build a website for a client, make sure the contract gives you a license to use the client's trademark in your work and also the right to use it on your own marketing materials to promote your portfolio of past work. As a default rule, your contract should ensure that you keep the intellectual property you create, especially if you think you might want to use parts of it again in later work. If a client wants to buy the underlying intellectual property in addition to the finished product, they should have to pay you a separate fee.

Bring your lawyer in early

For important contracts, consider bringing in your lawyer during the termsheet stage. I often help clients decide on what to ask for. Also, the earlier you involve your lawyer, the less likely you'll unwittingly agree to something disadvantageous. Lawyers have seen worst-case scenarios play out in real life, so they're good at spotting risks that you might not notice.

Lawyers provide good cover in negotiations, too. It's useful to be able to say, "My lawyer won't let me agree to that." Lawyers don't mind playing the tough guy in negotiations. You need to maintain a great working relationship with the people across the table, but you still need to get the terms you want, so split into a good cop/bad cop team and let your lawyer be the bad cop.

> **Quick Question: I have detailed emails about something we agreed to, but that term didn't end up in the final contract. What happens now?**
>
> Now you'll wish you'd read your contract more carefully before you signed. As we discussed in the chapters on email, recap emails are important to prevent miscommunication and to keep closed issues from re-opening during negotiations. However, once a contract is signed, those email discussions legally disappear (poof!). Always make sure the final contract pins down 100% of what you won in negotiations.
>
> When you spend so much time negotiating, don't give up in the final lap. Read every word of that contract, and don't be shy about raising questions if something is missing. It's your responsibility to make sure that every provision that benefits you makes it into the final version.

{Mistake 19}

Forgetting that real life is full of delays

The business terms usually set out what will happen if all goes well; the legal terms are generally more concerned with controlling the fallout if everything goes wrong. Hopefully you'll never have to call on your legal protections, but if you need them, you'll be glad they're there.

Negotiation of legal terms is usually done by marking up the actual contract. Once you start passing a draft contract back and forth, the final deal may feel very close. But don't forget: the devil is in the details. You might think you have a deal, until you read the first draft and realize the other side had unexpected ideas of what the agreement was. Even if the business terms seem to match, the legal side might not.

At this point, you should put on your pessimist hat and review the fine print carefully.

Deliverables aren't always delivered

The deliverables you discussed previously should be included in the contract in clear, easy-to-understand terms. Also, your contract should have some provisions about what happens if one party fails to meet the benchmarks. If Consultant Mark's social media campaign only yields a 15% increase in web traffic, even though he committed to delivering a 30% increase, do you get half your money back? All your money back? Maybe the first draft says that you get *none* of your money back, but Consultant Mark will re-do the work for free. If that's not acceptable to you, push back.

A lot of poorly drafted contracts go on at length about each party's responsibilities and make not a peep about what happens if one of the parties fails to follow through. A strong contract should lay out the events that could trigger a full refund, a partial refund, or re-performance of the work. Also, pay particular attention to what happens to money that has been prepaid, such as deposits and retainers.

In many circumstances, even a full refund won't be enough to cover you. For example, if Consultant Mark turns out to be a disappointment, you could just change the passwords and hire Consultant John instead. However, if you hire a construction company to fit out the space for your new business, and they run two months behind schedule, you could be out of pocket for a lot of money. You don't want to end up paying rent for space that you can't use, yet still be legally bound to pay the construction company its entire fee. Control these risks by setting up daily penalties ("liquidated damages") so that the construction company will pay for your rent and lost business if they fail to deliver as promised.

Similarly, if you need a prototype by a certain date to show to investors, or your restaurant's website needs to be up in time to coincide with ad time that you've already paid for, make sure your manufacturer and web designer is aware of the deadline and has some kind of financial penalty if they slip.

Look for limitations on liability

If a dry cleaner ruins your heirloom wedding gown, what will they owe you? Most likely, they'll owe you a $200 refund, if that's what you paid them, because there was a "limitation on liability" clause printed somewhere on your receipt or posted prominently at the drop-off site.

The limitation on liability is a crucial part of the fine print. If your construction contractor is paying daily penalties, for example, but the contract limits their liability in any way, they only have to pay up to that limit. Then they can sit around and soak up your rent for months.

If the other party can seriously damage your business (for example, by breaking your equipment or exposing your confidential information), be active about eliminating or increasing any liability caps that may be in the contract. Liability caps are usually given as a dollar figure or a percentage (100%, 150%, 200%) of the total amount that you paid the other party, and you won't recover more than that liability cap even if the other party causes a fire that burns down your entire data center.

When negotiating, aim for a figure that's fair for both sides: a dry cleaner would never accept wedding gowns for cleaning if they had unlimited liability, but a $500 cap would give them incentive to be extra careful.

Termination

Does the contract have a natural end date? Does it renew automatically? For example, maybe your contract with Consultant Mark runs for three-month terms that renew automatically. If you

aren't pleased with his level of attention, the easiest way to end the relationship is to give notice that you won't be renewing for the next quarter.

On the other hand, sometimes things can go so badly that you need to end mid-stream. For example, if you hire a web designer based on her great portfolio of past work, but her first draft makes your eyes bleed and she isn't responding to your requests for revision, what are your options? Your contract should spell out your right to terminate without cause (paired with a notice period of at least one month) and also your right to terminate with cause (paired with a much shorter notice period).

Pro Tip: Never sign a draft

This should not need to be said, yet it does. Never sign a draft! If a document isn't final, it should not have your signature.

Sometimes the other side will get impatient and try to make an end run by unilaterally deciding that negotiations are over. They might sign the document and send it to you "for your signature." As human beings, we have a strong urge to reciprocate, so it's easy to get confused – did we just agree that negotiations are over and this is the final contract? No, "we" did not!

Conversely, if the document is final and you are about to sign, it should not say "DRAFT" anywhere in the header, footer, title page, or body. That just causes confusion five or ten years down the road, when memory has faded and all that remains is an uncertain document.

How & When to
Hire a Lawyer

Seasoned business people always advise you to get "a lawyer you can trust." But how? And when?

Let's think about how to cadge some legal services for free, how to spot a good lawyer, and how to build a relationship that will last.

— — — — — — — — — — — — — — —

Not asking for a free consultation

Perhaps you are not reading this book for the pure love of beautiful knowledge. Very likely, you are scared of legal costs and hope to avoid hiring a lawyer altogether, if you can.

A lot of entrepreneurs try to DIY, and a lot of entrepreneurs regret it later – sometimes many years later, when they have lost their company. Here's a hard truth: legal services cost a lot because it takes an enormous amount of time to learn the language and practice of law. Technology and globalization have brought down the cost of many aspects of starting and running a business, but legal support costs just as much as it ever did.

Even lawyers hire lawyers

Law is a bit of a mirage because it looks as if it might be easy. For example, if you have only so much budget, you might be forced to either incorporate on your own or make your own website. If you don't have a technical background, it might seem as if you should hire someone to design the company website, since you don't know how to code but law looks as if it's written in English.

Legal drafting uses logic that's as rigorous as web coding, but it also uses words in highly specific, non-obvious ways. Legal English isn't really English at all. I know teenagers who've figured out the basics of HTML and CSS in a few weekends, but I don't know a single person who took the bar exam as a fun little hobby.

Moreover, legal language is *secretly* hard. If you make a mistake in your web code, your site will be obviously non-functional. That gives you an opportunity to edit your code until you get it right, so you can learn by trial and error.

Lawyers don't rely on trial and error. In fact, some of my clients are lawyers-turned-entrepreneurs. Lawyers hire lawyers because they know that if you make a legal mistake, you won't catch it until you're in legal trouble – and that will be a different kind of trial, and an entirely different magnitude of error.

How to ask for a free consultation

Rather than trying to learn the nuances of legal drafting from Google, try to come up with a useful budget. A good way to start is to avail yourself of some free consulting, which is little-known and surprisingly available. Lawyers are a bit snobby about their reputations, and the best firms tend not to advertise much. Think hard: have you *ever* seen a billboard for a corporate law firm? Instead, many excellent firms think about their marketing budget in terms of attorney time that they give away for free during half-hour consultations.

It's rude to take up someone's time unless there's a somewhat reasonable chance you'll end up working with them, so try to limit your attorney shopping. Three firms are probably plenty unless you talk to three people and genuinely feel uncomfortable with all of them.

Most lawyers prefer to be approached via email, since an unscheduled phone call can interrupt their workflow. A reasonable way to introduce yourself is: "I'm a business owner with a fairly lean budget. If you have half an hour, could I tell you a little bit about my business and get your thoughts on how best to plan for my legal needs in the upcoming year?" Take care not to misrepresent your budget. If you don't have any expectation to hire anyone for immediate work, make that clear up front. Many good lawyers can be surprisingly generous with their time, but not if they catch the scent of bad faith. (People who don't have time to take your call are not necessarily bad lawyers – they might be working 18 hours a day on existing clients.)

Practical tips on getting the most out of a consultation

If an attorney has time to schedule a call, fantastic! It's best to start with a brief introduction of your team (who you are, how long you've been working together). Try not to let personal introductions run too long; time is limited and your goal is to get some free legal advice. The bulk of your discussion should be based on the lawyer's thoughts on your elevator pitch. Here are some good questions to ask:

- In terms of legal risks (as opposed to business risks such as not being able to find a buyer for your product), does my business plan sound low risk, medium risk, or high risk? Attorneys have a sixth sense for risk and can tell you if there are lawsuits waiting to happen, or if your business model contains loopholes that might let customers eat and run.

- What are some ways I could control my risks? A good attorney will identify some of the strategies outlined in this book, such as updating your privacy policy or adding some protective terms to your standard invoices.

- What kinds of contracts do I need in order to lock in my company's value? For example, you probably need contracts with your primary customers, and it's wise to lock in certain vendors if you've negotiated a great deal. You might also need simple service agreements for your personnel or contracts that set up secondary revenue streams for advertisers or affiliate sales. A standard NDA is also helpful to have on hand.

- What kinds of laws might affect my business? For example, virtually all businesses have to be aware of their obligations regarding privacy and customer information. All internet video clips have to comply with copyright law and FCC regulations. Anything having to do with politics has to be aware of lobbying definitions and campaign finance filings. Your interviewees shouldn't be expected to know all the law, and especially not on the spot (there is more law in this country than can be learned in several lifetimes). This is just a good question to ask as a brainstorming exercise – take the results back to the law firm you choose to hire.

It may be helpful to send questions in advance, along with a brief summary of your business model. The idea is to find a thoughtful advisor, not a game show contestant who thinks fast on her feet.

Quick Question: Is my consultation confidential, even if I don't hire that attorney?

Yes. When you consult with an attorney for the purpose of potentially hiring her, your discussions are protected even though there is no attorney-client relationship yet. This confidentiality obligation activates automatically, so there's no need to sign a confidentiality agreement.

As a practical matter, it's important to indicate to each attorney which portions of the relevant information is confidential, since someone unfamiliar with your industry or your individual preferences might be unclear as to the boundary between public and private information. For example, some companies are secretive about their basic business model, while others broadcast it as part of their marketing strategy.

{Mistake 21}

Working with a lawyer you don't feel good about

It may not surprise you to learn that there are a number of bad lawyers in the world. In a few high profile cases, people have quite literally ended up on death row because their lawyer didn't care enough to interview key witnesses. In less dramatic cases, which unfortunately happen every day, people who hire bad lawyers can lose their homes, custody of their children, their life savings, or their businesses. Practicing law without a license carries criminal penalties because bad advice can be disastrous.

Of course, having a license does not make any lawyer a good lawyer. When people look at an attorney's website, most of what they see is (1) the brand name of the law school, (2) the total years of experience, and (3) a photo. None of these are exceptionally useful things to know.

A top law school is nice to see on a résumé, but everyone knows plenty of smart people who went to less famous schools. Experience is also nice to have, but Kim Jong Il's decades of experience as the leader of North Korea didn't improve his job performance. As an added note, it's risky to assume that older lawyers are more experienced – law is a popular second career, so there are plenty of people who take the bar exam later in life.

How to spot a good lawyer

When it comes to choosing a good lawyer, you should deploy the same interview skills that you would use on any potential hire. The hallmarks of a good lawyer include clear communication, good judgment, robust analysis, and an ethic of respect. Here are some things that you should see when you interact with your lawyer:

Clear communication. People who genuinely understand a subject can talk about it without big words and Latin phrases. A lawyer should be able to convey ideas with concrete examples and good business sense. You should come away from conversations feeling that you've learned something and have a clearer understanding of how to frame the issue, even if the ultimate answer is not yet clear.

Genuine listening. If you feel intimidated by your lawyer, he's not a good fit for you personally even if he knows his stuff. When you meet with a lawyer, you should feel comfortable speaking up and asking questions. Your lawyer should ask you a lot of questions about your business, and you should feel like you have good chemistry.

Creative solutions. Good lawyers actively look for solutions where middling lawyers just see problems. Sometimes there are win-win solutions to be found. For example, maybe you can rent-to-own your domain name with a small cash payment plus a percentage of your monthly revenues, since any activity you bring to the site will increase its search ranking even if your company chooses to release that domain name after a year. In other cases, there can be high-impact, low-cost fixes such as adding the "loser pays" clause to your terms and conditions. Good lawyers are always on the lookout for solutions as well as problems.

A real-world understanding of risk. One perennial complaint is that lawyers are too risk-averse. Your attorney should be highly *risk-aware*, but he should explain various options along the risk spectrum and leave the ultimate decisions up to you. If you ever find yourself leaving your attorney out of the loop on key legal decisions because you're worried that your attorney will overreact, then your attorney is not helping you manage risk effectively.

Team support. Many good lawyers belong to law firms so that they can get a second opinion, work in teams, and build pooled resources. There are great solo practitioners as well, but look for established solos who belong to a solid support network of other solos.

Alertness. Good lawyers take the time to understand your business, and they think of things (both problems and solutions) that haven't occurred to you yet. They ask the questions that you didn't think to ask.

Honesty about their own limitations. It would take several lifetimes to learn all the law of one state, much less all of them. Clients often expect lawyers to have all the answers at their fingertips, and those unrealistic expectations can put pressure on a lawyer to pontificate. Good lawyers are secure enough to say, "I don't know, that's a great question. Let me look into it and get back to you." Good lawyers are also humble enough to understand that you know your business better than he could ever know your business.

A good lawyer will be a valuable addition to your team for a long time to come, so look for someone whom you can see yourself working with over the long haul.

Quick Question: My attorney's shoddy work has cost me $150,000 in lost revenues and $35,000 in a lawsuit that I settled. Can I sue her for malpractice?

Yes in theory; no in practice. Although every client has a legal right to sue, the threshold of proof is nearly impossible to meet.

Let's think about medical malpractice as a comparison. Your doctor doesn't have to be the best, most conscientious doctor in the world. Maybe your doctor got the occasional D in medical school and skipped a few classes. If the rule were "a doctor must be as good as the industry average," then, mathematically, 49% of all doctors would be malpracticing at any given time.

To win a medical malpractice case, your doctor has to fall below the acceptable minimum standard, from a low D to an outright F, such as by amputating the wrong toe.

Since lawyers wrote the law, the standard for attorneys is even lower. To win an attorney malpractice claim, you have to prove that you lost your court case *because of* your attorney. For example, there have been multiple cases where defendants were sentenced to death because their state-appointed attorneys literally took naps during trial. On appeal, judges have sometimes ruled that the naps made no difference because the defendant might have received the same sentence even if the attorney had done his job.

There's also a famous case where an attorney drafted a will incorrectly, and the judge ruled that even though the attorney had made a clear error, the disinherited heirs didn't have legal standing to sue the attorney because they were not named in the will. Only the client (i.e., the deceased) had legal standing to sue.

In practice, the only cases that you can expect to win are those involving black-and-white rules, such as when an attorney misses a filing deadline. For most other situations, you can file a complaint with the state bar association, which can provide warnings to future clients, but it's unlikely you'll get any compensation for the money you lost.

Miscommunicating
with your lawyer

To develop a great relationship with your lawyer, you have to hold up your end of the bargain. Let's think about some ways to encourage an outstanding working relationship with the thoughtful, communicative attorney you found after shopping around.

How professionals talk about legal budgets

Legal fees, of course, are one of the biggest issues in attorney-client relationships. Both attorneys and clients can find this topic uncomfortable. There are unstoppable market forces at play, so attorney time will always cost more than marketer time, designer time, accountant time, or anything other than supermodel time. Basically, good legal talent is a hot commodity. As long as Fortune500 companies are willing to pay $500-$1,000 an hour in order to hire top lawyers, the most prestigious law firms will compete for top talent by offering Wall-Street-sized salaries. Since law is a talent-driven industry, firms of all sizes have to pay competitive compensation, or their best attorneys will fly away. All that payroll adds up to a lot of cost, which ultimately lands on the client.

One professional way to control your budget is to explain politely and candidly, "Our legal budget is strictly capped at *x* dollars at this time. You are welcome to let me know your recommend-ations for future work, but right now we aren't able to authorize more than *x* dollars of work." It's also possible to ask if you can spread the payments out over time. Discussion about fees should always happen *before* you retain a firm, not after they have provided services.

Either a law firm can meet your price point, or it can't. If no reputable law firm can meet your price point, you may be setting an unrealistic expectation on the amount of work your case requires.

I once grumbled to a doctor friend that my doctor never seemed to spend much time with me. "Do you really think," she responded, "that your face time with your doctor is the only time that she spends on you?" I was embarrassed to realize that *of course* my doctor spends time reviewing my file right before she comes in the door, is looking up details on medications when she leaves in the middle of my examination, and spends time making notes in my file after I leave. Then she has to deal with insurance billing codes. What I see is just a fraction of her workday, just as what my legal clients see is a fraction of my workday.

Being a good client is about more than just paying the bills on time, however. As with any service industry, the better you are at being served, the better your service.

How to be a good client

As a practicing attorney, here are some things that clients can do to help their attorneys deliver great service:

Be educated. Just as a doctor relies on you to describe your symptoms accurately, your lawyer has to rely on you to get the facts of the situation, as well as honest assessments of the what-ifs down the road. You don't need to go to medical school to be a good patient, but it definitely helps if you have a basic understanding that antibiotics cannot cure the common cold. At my firm, we love working with clients who are always learning.

Communicate clearly. The gold standard in all business communication is to be clear, concise, and relevant. I would add one more: ego-free. The best clients neither steamroll with arrogance nor quiver with insecurity. Be receptive to advice, but also speak up when you have questions! For example, imagine that you're explaining the case history but your attorney seems totally uninterested in a part that you thought was most important. Should you assume it's unimportant and drop it, or should you keep bringing up the troubling fact in hopes that it will catch your attorney's attention? Neither. You should simply ask, "Is it relevant that _____?" What an easy way to solve the mystery.

It's usually best to designate one person at your company to be the official point of communication with your lawyer. Routing questions through a single person can save on duplication of labor (and therefore fees). It also helps grow a steady, communicative relationship.

Be clear about expectations. What's the timeline? How much is at stake? If you are idly considering a new project, you might want an unresearched gut reaction on whether any major issues seem to jump out. Say so. If you are looking for a summary of the potential legal issues to insert into a formal proposal, that will take a few more hours. If you're gearing up for a major investment, ask for a fully researched, reliable analysis before you jump. The amount of legal certainty you ask for should roughly match up with the amount of money at stake. (Conversely, if you ask for a lightweight analysis, it's not fair to be upset if it turns out to be wrong or incomplete. Law is complicated. If you hold off-the-cuff errors against your lawyer, you train him to be more risk-averse next time.)

Keep your lawyer in the loop. Often, people wait until a deal is almost done to mention it to their lawyer. Attorneys hate this: there's often a busload of problems that no one has thought of, deadlines are looming, and now the lawyer looks like a naysaying obstructionist. Contrary to popular belief, most lawyers don't enjoy being party poopers. If consulted early in the process, a good lawyer can almost always come up with a solution that will let you do what you want to do, yet structure the risk in an efficient manner. Before committing funds to a new project, check with legal to discuss risk management. When negotiating a deal, get legal involved at the termsheet stage. Everyone comes out happier.

Praise in public. Everyone loves public praise, but attorneys fairly starve for it. As a business matter, law is a high-touch industry, yet many of the best lawyers are introverts who loathe salesmanship. As a result, word-of-mouth referrals are priceless, and firms go the extra mile for clients who are influencers within the community. If you are happy with your law firm, show them that you are appreciative (and well-connected) by copying them on emails when you recommend them to people.

And of course, be nice. If you treat your restaurant waiter with courtesy and warmth, you are more likely to be greeted with a smile next time. Law is a service profession too, and sometimes quite a stressful one, so remember that your lawyer is a person. A reliable lawyer will be of immeasurable help in the long term, so invest the time to find one you can work with, and then invest in the relationship so that it can grow over time, just like your business.

{Thanks}

Even a small book takes a big effort from a lot of people.
From the first outline to the final proofread, Leah Goodman was
the perfect editor. Norwic, a delightful artist to work with,
performed miracles in transforming heavy-duty legal concepts into
light-hearted illustrations full of wit and charm.

I absolutely love the eye-catching cover design created by
Jane Chu, and I can't thank Skye enough for his help in the last leg
of the journey. Another big thank you goes out to Sarah, Barbara,
and Serena for their support and encouragement as my test
readers. I've been so fortunate to have all of you on my team.

{Notes}

{New Questions}

About the Author

Sue Wang is an attorney in Washington, DC. Her areas of focus include project finance, mergers & acquisitions, and advising closely held companies. She has a particular interest in renewable energy and clean technology.

Ms. Wang earned her B.A. from Rice University and her J.D. from the University of Michigan Law School in Ann Arbor, where she served as a contributing editor of the *Michigan Law Review*. She has been featured as a presenter at many entrepreneurial events.